GW01459107

South Korean Desserts

Korean Desserts and Sweets from Traditional to Modern

Copyright © 2021

All rights reserved.

DEDICATION

Contents

Korean Shaved Ice Dessert

Ingredients

400 g ice cubes (0.9 pounds)

2 Tbsp sweetened red bean paste (or more to taste)

2 Tbsp sweetened condensed milk (or more to taste)

16 mini sweet rice cakes (mochi)

80 g strawberry (2.8 ounces), chopped

45 g kiwi (1.6 ounces), thinly sliced

45 g blueberry (1.6 ounces)

45 g pineapple (1.6 ounces), chopped

Instructions

Put the ice blocks into a food processor (or shaved ice machine if you have one). Grind the ice (for about 20 seconds) until it has a smooth texture.

Place the shaved ice into a chilled serving bowl. Top up with your choice of fruit, red bean paste, mochi. Garnish with sweetened condensed milk.

Serve.

Fish-Shaped Bread

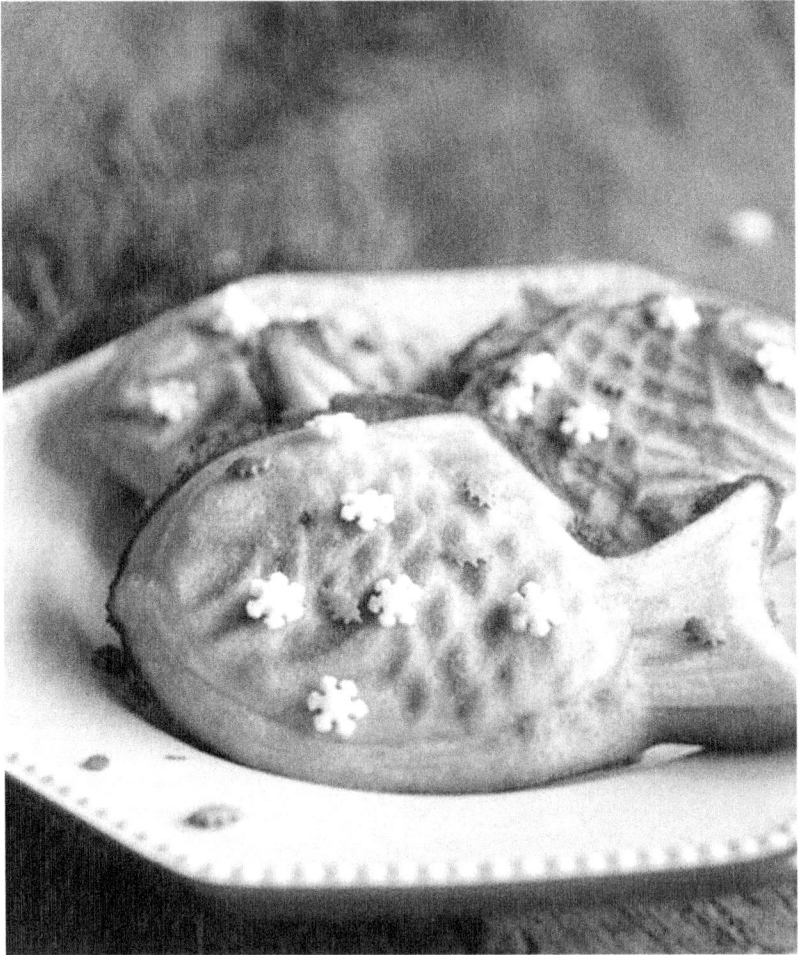

Ingredients

75 g all purpose flour

35 g sweet rice flour (mochiko)

1/2 tsp baking soda

1/2 tsp baking powder

1 egg

1 Tbsp sugar

135 ml milk whole or low fat, 135 ml = 1/2 cup + 1 Tbsp

1 tsp vegetable oil

1/8 tsp pinch of salt

For filling

200 g canned sweet red beans or sweet red bean paste 7 oz can

1 Tbsp melted butter or 1 Tbsp veg. oil (for the pan)

Instructions

Mix all dry ingredients together.

Whisk egg and milk separately in a bowl.

Mix dry ingredients and wet altogether.

Heat the bungeoppang pan (closed) on medium heat on both sides until water sizzles on both sides. (about 1 min on each side)

Open the pan and coat inside of each fish mold (4 molds in all) with butter or oil. pastry brush works best.

Lower heat to low and pour batter into one side of the molds (2 fishes) only about 1/3 full. Just enough to cover the eye of the fish.

Quickly spoon red beans into the center of the fish. About 2 tsp full is good. More or less to taste.

Pour batter on top of the read beans to fully cover the half fish mold.

Bungeoppang pan with batter and sweet red bean filling in pan

Close the pan and turn over.

Bring heat a little higher to medium-low.

Cook on each side for 2 - 2:30 min.

You can open after 2 min to check the doneness. Cook more if it's not yet brown.

When brown on both sides, transfer to a plate and let it cool for few min.

The red bean filling can be EXTREMELY HOT so please be careful.

Korean Sweet Rice Punch

Ingredients

6 oz (170 g) Yeotgireum (Coarse Malted Barley Powder) approximately 1 cup

1.75 L (7 ½) cups water

1/2 cup uncooked rice

2/5 cup (80 g) sugar This is on the less sweet side. You may add a few more tablespoons, up to ¼ cup more sugar, to taste.

Instructions

Rice. Make the rice in a rice cooker. Use a bit less water than usual to produce a drier rice.

Malted Flour.

Pour the coarse malted barley into a large bowl. Soak the barley in water. Follow one of the steps below.

Option 1 (Preferred): Place malted barley in cheesecloth. Soak in large pot of water. Massage the malted barley several times during the one hour. The water will get milky. Strain and discard the bag.

Option 2: If you don't have a cheesecloth - place malted barley in a large pot of water to soak. Gently massage the malted barley several times during the one hour. The water will get milky. Strain through a sieve and make sure to squeeze out all the water. Discard the malted barley.

Rest the milky water for about 30 minutes to an hour to separate the sediments to the bottom of the bowl. Gently pour the milky water into the rice cooker.

Add about 1 Tbsp of sugar to the rice cooker. (This will make the fermentation process go slightly faster).

Don't add the sentiments at the bottom of the bowl into the rice cooker.

Place the rice cooker on the "keep warm" option for about 4-5 hours, or until 4-5 rice granules rice to the top.

Pour the milky liquid from the rice cooker into a large pot. Add the rest of the sugar. Boil on medium heat for about 10 minutes. Skim off any foam that floats at the top.

Once the sugar has dissolved into the milky liquid, set aside and bring to room temperature and refrigerate until cold.

Korean Sweet Pancakes

Ingredients

Dough

1 cup lukewarm water

2 Tablespoons sugar

2 teaspoons active dry yeast

1 Tablespoon vegetable oil

½ teaspoon salt

2 cups all-purpose flour

Filling

½ cup brown sugar

4 Tablespoons chopped walnuts

1 teaspoon cinnamon

Instructions

In a large mixing bowl or the bowl of a stand mixer, stir together the lukewarm water, sugar, yeast, oil and salt. Let the yeast proof for about

5 minutes until it starts to get foamy.

Add the flour to the yeast mixture and knead with the mixer until smooth.

Cover dough tightly with plastic wrap and allow it to rise for 1 hour at room temperature until the dough has doubled in size. Coat your hand lightly in cooking spray and punch down the dough to remove gas bubbles, then cover again and let the dough rise another 20 minutes.

During the last rise, mix together the filling ingredients in a small bowl.

When the dough is ready, turn it out onto a floured surface and coat your hands with flour (it's a very sticky dough to work with). Divide into 8 equal-sized pieces and shape into balls.

Working with one dough ball at a time, flatten it out and mound about a tablespoon of the filling in the center. Then pinch the edges of the disc together up around the filling, enclosing it completely in the center of the ball of dough as seen in the pictures. Repeat with the remaining balls of dougha and filling. You may need to re-flour your hands between dough balls if the dough starts sticking too much.

Heat a large pan over medium heat. When hot, add a little oil (about 2 tablespoons) to the pan and let that heat up as well. When the oil is hot, place a dough ball in it, with the sealed area down and cook until lightly golden brown on the bottom (just about 30 seconds), then flip. Using a large, flat spatula, press down on the hotteok to flatten it into a wide disc and cook until the bottom is golden brown.

Flip the hotteok one last time and reduce the heat to low. Cover the pan with a lid and cook for another minute or so, just until the bottom is completely golden brown and the filling inside is melted and syrupy.

You can cook more than one hotteok at a time if your pan is large enough. Just make sure to leave enough space between each dough ball so that it can be pressed flat into a disc.

Serve hot!

Pepero Cake

Ingredients

1.5 packets Pepero or Pocky (30 sticks)

1/3 swiss roll cake (about 9cm in length)

1/4 cup heavy cream

1 cup baking chocolate (155 g / 5.5 ounces)

1/4 cup pistachio nuts (in shells)

Instructions

Cut the swiss roll cake into three pieces (about 3cm thickness) and set aside.

Cut/break Pepero sticks to separate the chocolate coated part and not coated part (yellow handles) and set aside. (We will only use the chocolate coated part for the recipe.)

Shell the pistachio nuts, coarsely chop them and set aside.

Add the chocolate into a bowl and melt it by microwaving it. Once the chocolate is melted, add the heavy cream into the chocolate bowl and mix them well.

Stack the swiss roll cake and pour the chocolate mixture on the outer layer of the cake. Spread it with a bread knife.

Stick the Pepero around the cake wall and decorate the top of the cake with the pistachio nuts. Serve.

Sweet Red Bean Porridge

Ingredients

For the porridge

1 cup pat팥 (aka adzuki beans)

1 tablespoon glutinous rice flour (aka sweet rice powder) Chapssal garu (찹쌀가루) or mochiko

2 tablespoons sugar (or light brown sugar)

1 tablespoon honey (use more sugar to taste if unavailable)

½ teaspoon salt

For the rice cake balls

1/2 cup glutinous rice powder (aka sweet rice powder) Chapssal garu (찹쌀가루) or mochiko

2 teaspoons sugar

pinch salt

4 tablespoons boiling hot water

Optional garnish

1 tablespoon pine nuts

4 to 6 boiled chestnuts (or canned)

1/4 to 1/2 teaspoon cinnamon powder

Instructions

For the porridge

Discard broken or rotten beans and rinse the beans. In a large pot, add the beans with 4 cups of water. Bring it to a boil, uncovered, over medium high heat. Reduce the heat to medium and boil for 5 min.

Drain the beans.

Return the beans to the pot with 4 cups of fresh water. Cover, and simmer over medium low heat until the beans are very soft and easily breakable, about 1 to 1-½ hours. Turn off the heat, and let the beans cool in the cooking liquid.

Puree the beans along with the cooking liquid until velvety smooth. You may need to do this step in two batches. Add some water if the bean puree gets too thick.

Return the bean puree to the pot. Mix one tablespoon of the sweet rice powder in ½ cup of water, and pour into the pot. Stir in the salt, sugar and honey.

Simmer over medium low heat, uncovered, stirring frequently, for about 10 minutes. Adjust the thickness of the porridge by adding more water if necessary.

For the rice cake balls

Mix the rice powder, sugar and salt in a bowl. Stir in the boiling hot water with a spoon. When cool enough to handle, knead by hand until a dough is formed. Shape the dough into a 3/4-inch thick cylinder.

Cut into (or pinch off) 3/4-inch pieces. Roll each piece between the palms to make a small ball.

Bring a pot of water to a boil. Add the rice cake balls. Cook until all the balls float. Transfer to a large bowl with cold water to cool.

To serve:

Ladle some porridge into a serving bowl. Serve hot with a few rice balls and optional garnishes.

Creamy Red Bean Popsicles

INGREDIENTS

1/2 cup dried red beans (or 1 1/2 cups cooked, unsweetened red beans)

1 cup whole milk

1/2 cup condensed milk

INSTRUCTIONS

Add red beans into a medium-sized bowl and add water to cover, at least by 1 inch. Soak until the beans are rehydrated (3 hours at a minimum, up to overnight).

Drain soaked red beans and transfer to a medium-sized pot. Add cold water to cover by 2 inches. Cook over medium high heat until brought to a simmer. Immediately turn to low heat. Simmer covered until the red beans turn tender without breaking apart, about 50 minutes (*Footnote 1). Rinse the red beans with tap water to cool and drain.

(Optional) Separate and save 1/4 cup whole red beans to add into the Popsicles for texture, if desired.

Combine the cooked red beans and milk in a blender (I used a

Vitamix). Start at low speed and increase to high, blending for 30 seconds if you like a texture with tiny pieces of crushed beans, and 1 minute for a smoother texture.

Add condensed milk. Start at low speed and increase to medium, blending for 5 seconds, until the condensed milk is just incorporated.

Transfer the mixture into Popsicle molds and place them in the freezer for 30 minutes, until the mixture thickens. Meanwhile, soak the Popsicle sticks in water. (*Footnote 2)

Insert the Popsicle sticks, keeping them as straight as possible. Return the Popsicle molds to the freezer for another 4 to 5 hours, until the Popsicles have solidified.

To remove a Popsicle, run the mold under warm water for 3 to 5 seconds, and then gently pull the Popsicle out and enjoy!

Korean Kkwabaegi Donuts

Ingredients

240 grams Bread Flour

60 grams Glutinous Rice Flour

30 grams Sugar

4 grams Salt

140 grams Milk

8 grams Instant Dry Yeast

40 grams Egg

40 grams Butter (Salted or Unsalted, leave out at room temperature)

Topping

Few Tablespoons of Sugar

Instructions

Make Dough

Take out a large mixing bowl. Place 240 grams of bread flour through a sift. Then sift 60 grams of glutinous rice flour. Make two holes in the flour. Add in the sugar (30 grams) and salt (4 grams) into each. Then cover each hole up.

Now briefly place your milk on the stove or in the microwave so that it turns WARM. Do not make the milk HOT - just warm! Then add-in the Instant Dry Yeast (8 grams) into the milk and give it a stir. Next, crack 1 whole egg into a separate bowl. Give it a thorough whisk and measure out exactly 40 grams. Pour the 40 grams of egg into the milk mixture. Give it another stir!

At this step, if you have a stand mixer (with a dough hook) - use it! If not, we'll knead by hand. Slowly pour the milk mixture into the dry flour mixture and stir it around with the other hand. Once it's all poured in, continue to stir. The flour will start to crumble-up and lump together. At this point, use both hands to knead the dough until it doesn't stick to your fingers (~5-7 minutes).

Next, you want to use butter that's been sitting out at room temperature - it's easier to mix in. Place 40 grams of room-temperature butter into the dough and mix it in with your hands. At first, it will feel quite nasty - but don't worry, it will get all mixed in! Keep kneading until you don't feel the stickiness of the butter on your hands and you see the dough changing colors to a faint yellow (~8-10 minutes).

First Rise

Now place the dough into a mixing bowl. Cover with plastic wrap. We will then allow the dough to rise in a warm area. If you'll use your oven to proof, turn the light on and then place-in a cup filled with boiling water. Let it rise for 40-50 minutes.

Make Twisted Donut Shape

After 50 minutes, take off the plastic wrap. You'll see that the dough has risen. Release the gas by giving the puffed-up dough a few gentle punches with your fist. Then gently re-mold the dough back into a ball shape. Use a knife and quarter the dough in half. Then cut those pieces in half again. And those pieces in half once more. Then use a scale to measure out 60 grams of dough for each piece. You should end up with 8-9 equal pieces.

Use your palm to roll each dough piece in one direction (as shown in the video) - into the shape of small cocoons. Afterwards, dip your fingers in some water and flick it over the dough so it doesn't dry out. Cover the cocoons with plastic wrap or a cheese cloth... so it doesn't dry out before you start the ext step.

Now, let's make the donut shape. Grab one dough piece at a time and roll it back-and-forth with your palm. We want them to get around 25 cm in length (doesn't have to be exact). Then use both palms to roll one end, upward and the other end, downward. This will create some tension in the dough. Lift it up and bring the two ends together - and the dough should naturally twist into shape. (You can also use hand to help make the twist as well).

2nd Rise

Place the twisted donuts onto a sheet tray, lined with wax paper. Place into a warm oven and let it rise for a second time. Set a timer for 30 minutes for this last rise.

After 30 minutes, take the donut out of the oven. You'll see that the donuts have puffed up! It's time to fry them.

Fry Donut

Take out a large pot or wok. Place in vegetable oil. Turn on heat and bring up to 180°C / 350°F. Once its hot, place the donuts into the oil and fry until both sides turn golden brown. Flip them as necessary while they cook.

Place onto a cooling rack for 1-2 minutes.

Take out a plastic bag and fill with sugar. Place the fried donuts inside and give them a gentle shake.

Korean Tea Cookies

Ingredients

1 cup roasted sesame seeds (110 g / 4 oz) or 1/2 cup sesame seed powder (white or black sesame seeds)

1/8 tsp sea salt or more to taste

honey syrup (makes extra – use 4 tsp to 2 Tbs of syrup per 1/2 cup ground powder)

1/2 cup rice syrup (조청 jocheong)

3/4 cup honey1/2 cup sugar (7 oz / 100 g)

2 Tbsp water

Instructions

If your sesame seeds are not roasted, roast your sesame seeds in pan for 3-5 minutes on medium heat. Stirring often so they don't burn.

Melt sugar and water in a pot on medium heat. Once sugar is all melted, add honey and rice syrup. Raise heat to medium high and stir often and bring to boil. Turn off heat and let it cool. Do not over cook

Finely grind sesame seeds in a blender. The longer you blend, the finer it will be.

In a bowl, add the sesame seed powder and sprinkle sea salt on top.

Add 1 Tbs + 1 tsp of the honey syrup to 1/2 cup sesame seed powder and mix well. It should become pretty lumpy and hold shape when you form it in your hand. Similar to play-doh consistency.

Take a little bit of the dough and roll into a ball. Raise the mold by inserting the bar so the dough can be pressed into the mold.

Press the ball into each mold and make sure it is filled to the top to be flush with the frame.

Once the molds are filled, take out the spacer and push the upper frame down.

The cookies will now stick out (protrude) from the mold and you can gently remove each cookie.

Korean Honey Pastry

Ingredients

For dough

3 cup all purpose flour (medium-protein flour)

1/3 cup sesame oil

1/3 cup soju

1/3 cup honey

1/4 cup chopped pine nuts1/4 tsp salt (optional – original recipe omits salt)

For Syrup

1 cup rice syrup

1 cup honey

2 cup water

1 Tbsp ginger

Instructions

Prepare oil for frying. Note for Yakgwa, we want to start frying at a low temperature.

Make syrup by mixing rice syrup, honey and water in a sauce pan or frying pan. Heat on medium heat, stirring occasionally. Once it boils, turn the heat off and add the chopped ginger, mix and set it aside.

In a large mixing bowl, add flour (add salt – optional) and then sesame oil. Mix the flour with the oil by rubbing the mixture thoroughly with your hands, until you feel the oil is all blended in with the flour.

Mix the Soju and honey in a separate cup/bowl until the honey is all dissolved.

Pour soju/honey mixture into the flour mixture and gently press the dough to form a ball.

Divide dough in half. Roll out one half of the dough into 1/4 to 1/3 inch thick rectangular shape. Cut the dough into 1 inch wide strips and then cut the strips at an angle to make diamond shapes.

Yakgwa is fried in 2 different temperatures and this what makes it tricky. For the first part, oil should be around 265° F (130°C). Yakwa will slowly rise to the top.

For the second part, when all the pieces have risen to the top, raise the heat to medium high to reach normal frying temperature . Continue frying until Yakgwa turns rich brown in color.

When Yakgwa pieces turn rich dark brown, removec from oil and let oil drain in a colander lined with paper towel.

Soak fried Yakgwa in prepared ginger honey syrup.

Leave for few min until it has soaked up all the syrup, take it out of the syrup and place onto a plate.

Sprinkle top with chopped pine nuts while it is still wet so the nuts will stick to it.

Baking Soda Cookie

INGREDIENTS

2 Tbs Sugar

1/8 tsp Baking Soda

DIRECTIONS

Melt down the sugar in a ladle by holding it over the stove in the kitchen at medium low heat and continuously stirring so the sugar doesn't burn.

Once the sugar completely melts, add in a little bit of baking soda as you continue to stir. When the mixture fully expands and the color changes to light brown, remove it from the heat. If it starts to turn into a darker brown, you have started to burn the mixture.

Quickly pour the mixture onto the tray and press the cookie treat down with the stamp and the cookie cutout. Quickly lift the stamp and pull the cookie cutter out of the cookie.

Once completely cooled, scrape the sugar treat off the tray with the scraper.

Repeat for more sugar cookies and enjoy!

Sweet Potato Rice Donuts

INGREDIENTS

3/4 lb sweet potato cooked and peeled

2 cup sweet rice flour (chapssal-garu) glutenous rice flour

1/3 cup all-purpose flour can omit for gluten-free

1/3 cup sugar

1 tsp salt

1/2 tsp baking powder

1-1 1/3 cup hot milk

Oil for frying

For the cinnamon sugar

1/2 cup granulated sugar

1 tsp cinnamon

INSTRUCTIONS

Combine flours, sugar, baking powder, and salt in a large bowl.

Mash sweet potato and add to the flour mixture and rub together until the flours become fine crumbs.

Slowly add hot milk (1/4 cup of milk each time) to the mixture and mix together with a spoon first, then using hand bring the dough together to form a ball shape. The amount of milk depends on the moisture level of your potatoes. It should resemble the bread dough consistency.

Make them into 1" balls with the dough. Set aside and cover with a towel.

Heat oil in a wok or fryer over medium low temperature. Drop a few dough balls and start rolling with a metal utensil to brown them evenly, about 5 minutes. Make sure your oil is not too hot. About 145°C is ideal temperature.

Transfer the donuts to a plate lined with paper towel to remove extra oil on the surface. Roll the donuts in cinnamon sugar and coat evenly. Serve warm or at room temperature.

Korean Pear Dessert

Ingredients

1 Korean pear (490 g / 1 pound), peeled

3 cups water

15 g ginger (0.5 ounces), peeled, thinly sliced

2 Tbsp sugar or honey

24 black peppercorns (optional)

Some pine nuts (optional) to garnish

Instructions

Put the sliced ginger into a pot and add the water. Boil over medium high heat until rolling boiling (7 to 8 mins).

(At the same time as step 1) Cut the pears into wedge shapes (about 8 pieces). Push through the black peppercorns on the back of the pears (typically 3 peppercorns per slice). You may want to use a chopstick or an equivalent tool to push them deep, so that they don't fall out. Though, if you don't like this additional peppercorn flavour, it can be omitted.

Discard the ginger from step 1. Add the sliced pears and sugar / honey into the pot. Boil them over low heat for about 10 mins.

Remove the pot from the heat and cool down. Chill in the fridge for a few hours. Garnish the drink with some pine nuts before serving. Serve cold or warm.

Korean Watermelon Punch

Ingredients

2 cups watermelon, balled or cubed

1-1/2 cups honeydew melon

12 - 16 rice cake balls (gyeongdan)- optional

2 cups ginger ale

3 tablespoons Korean drinking vinegar or pomegranate or cranberry juice1 tablespoon pine nuts for garnish - optional

Optional rice cake balls:

1/2 cup glutinous rice powder aka sweet rice powder

2 teaspoons sugar

pinch salt

4 tablespoons boiling hot water

Instructions

Make optional rice cake balls (recipe below). Scoop out watermelon and honeydew with a melon-baller. (Or, cut into about 1-inch cubes.) Place them in a large bowl along with any juice from the fruits.

Add the ginger ale and the drinking vinegar (or pomegranate or cranberry juice) to the fruits. Stir gently. Taste the drink and adjust acidity and/or sweetness by adding more drinking vinegar (or juice and/or sugar).

Optional rice cake balls

Mix the rice powder, sugar and salt in a bowl. Mix in the boiling hot water with a spoon. When cool enough to handle, knead by hand until a dough is formed.

Shape the dough into a 3/4-inch thick cylinder. Cut into (or pinch of3/4-inch pieces. Roll each piece between the palms to make a small ball.

Bring a pot of water to a boil. Add the rice cake balls. Cook until all the balls float. Transfer to a large bowl with cold water to cool. Drain.

Korean Honey Bread

Ingredients:

2 inch thick unsliced white or wheat bread

honey butter

cinnamon sugar

maple syrup or chocolate syrup

peanut butter spread

whipped cream

fruits (cherries, kiwi, strawberry etc)

Directions:

1. Microwave 2 tbsp honey and butter for 20 seconds.

2. Cut 1 inch thick grid-like patterns across the bread. Drizzle top with honey butter mixture until the bread gets well soaked.

3. Sprinkle top with cinnamon sugar. Toast in the oven for 10 minutes until lightly browned.

4. Transfer bread to a plate. Spread top with peanut butter. Drizzle with maple or chocolate syrup.

5. Pipe whipped cream rosettes or swirls on top of the bread. Garnish with sliced fruit.

6. Dust with cocoa or confectionery sugar.

7. Enjoy! Happy eating!

Korean Scorched Rice

Ingredients

1½ cup leftover cooked rice at least a day old and cold

Equipments

Parchment paper

Air fryer

Instructions

Preheat air fryer to 400 degrees F.

Cut a parchment paper so it fits on the air fryer tray.

Add rice on the parchment paper in a single layer about ½ inch thick. You may need to break up the rice a bit to do this.

Cook in the air fryer for 9-10 minutes if you want it slightly chewy with a crispy layer, or 11-12 minutes for an ultra crunchy texture.

Remove from the air fryer (it should be in one large piece), then cool for a few minutes.

Break it up with your hands and enjoy on its own, with kimchi, sugar, furikake, sriracha mayo, or however you want to enjoy it!

Pan-Fried Sweet Rice Cakes

Ingredients

1 cup glutinous rice flour (sweet rice flour)

¼ teaspoon kosher salt

½ cup hot boiling water

Edible flowers

2 to 3 tablespoons vegetable oil

Honey (or homemade syrup)

Directions

Make the dough and shape the rice cakes

Combine glutinous rice flour and salt in a bowl.

Add the hot water a little by little and mix well with a wooden spoon (or rice scoop) until the dough has cooled enough that you can knead it by hand.

Knead the dough until it's smooth for about 1 to 2 minutes, then divide it into 10 equal-sized pieces. Roll each piece into a ball.

Keep them covered with a piece of plastic wrap so they don't dry out.

Press each rice cake ball into a disc about 2½ inches (6 to 7 cm) in diameter and put them on a large platter or on the cutting board.

Pan-fry

Heat up a large non-stick skillet over medium heat. Add the vegetable oil, swirling the skillet to coat the surface. Once it's heated up, turn the heat down low. The key to beautiful hwajeon is to keep them white by pan-frying over low heat.

Put the uncooked rice cakes on the skillet and cook them for a few minutes.

When the bottoms are slightly crispy, turn them over and flatten them out with a spatula. Cook a few more minutes and turn them over.

Place edible flowers on the top of each rice cake, then flip them over and press them down for 1 second so that the flower sticks to the cake.

Cook each one and put them on a serving plate.

Serve

Drizzle some honey on top of the rice cakes.

Serve with tea as a dessert or snack.

Rice Cake Skewers

INGREDIENTS

1 lb rice cakes fresh or frozen (chilled), about3-inch long pieces

2 tbsp canola oil

3 tbsp Korean chili paste (gochujang)

2 tbsp ketchup

1/2 tbsp minced garlic

1 tbsp strawberry jam or sweet chili sauce

1 tbsp honey

1-2 tbsp water

dashes of freshly cracked pepper

2 tbsp finely chopped nuts of your choice

INSTRUCTIONS

Insert 3-4 fresh rice cakes through each skewer. If using frozen rice cakes, blanch the cakes in hot water until soften, wipe off the moisture with paper towel, then insert the skewers.

In a small bowl, combine chili paste, ketchup, garlic, jam (and/or sweet chili sauce), honey, water, and black pepper; mix well . Pour the sauce in a small skillet and boil for 1 minute until slightly thicken. Set aside.

Heat oil in a skillet over medium heat and fry the rick cake skewers until crisp and bubbly on the surface, about 2-3 minutes on each side. Brush with the sauce and sprinkle the chopped nut over.

Serve warm or at room temperature.

Caramelized Sweet Potatoes

Ingredients

2 large sweet potatoes about 1¾-2 pounds total

¼ cup water

1 tablespoon extra virgin olive oil

1 tablespoon butter

2 tablespoons honey

1 teaspoon ground coriander

½ teaspoon kosher salt more to taste

fresh finely chopped parsley for garnish if desired.

US Customary - Metric

Instructions

Peel sweet potatoes and cut into ½-inch cubes*.

Combine all ingredients in a large skillet with a lid. With cover off, bring mixture to a boil over medium-high heat. Stir well. Reduce heat to a maintain a steady simmer, then cover and cook for 3 minutes.

Remove cover, increase heat to medium and cook, stirring occasionally, until liquid has evaporated and potatoes are tender, golden and caramelized. This will take around 4-6 minutes. If liquid evaporates and potatoes are not tender, add a few tablespoons of water and continue cooking and stirring till tender. You want them tender, but not mushy.

Garnish with fresh, chopped parsley, if desired.

Crispy Accordion Potatoes

Ingredients

4 potatoes Yukon Gold, Maris Piper, Russet, Charlotte, etc.

2 Tbsp olive oil or butter/ dairy-free butter

1/2 tsp salt

Toppings (check the main post for tons of options)

ketchup

parsley

Instructions

Step 1: Cut the potatoes

Wash and scrub your potatoes well then slice them lengthways about 1/2-3/4-inch in thickness.

The thicker your pieces, the less crispy the center will be. However, cut it too thin and the accordion potato pattern won't work. Mine were around 3/4-inch for this, though I think 1/2-inch would yield crispier results.

For Thin Slices

To cut the accordion potato pattern, place a potato slice vertically, between two skewers (refer to pictures).

Slice the potato horizontally (sideways) every 1/4-inch or so – try to be reasonably even about it.

Flip over the potato slice and repeat the process, this time slicing diagonally*. Try to cut the same 1/4-inch or so apart, though.

Gently pull the potato from both ends to loosen up the pattern and twist it lightly in your hands. Then push it back together and push a skewer going up through the middle of the slice.

For Accordion boxes

If you want to make the more 'detailed' accordion, then you can do this with a square (rather than sliced) bit of potato.

Follow similar steps by placing the potato between the skewers and slicing first horizontally, then flipping over and slicing diagonally.

Step 2: Soak the potato slices

Soak the potato slices in water for 10 minutes. This will reduce some of the potatoes' excess starch and allow them to become crispier when baking.

Use boiling water and soak the potatoes for 20 minutes if you want to par-cook the potato and reduce the baking time.

Once soaked, pat the potatoes thoroughly dry with a kitchen towel. If they're not dry, they won't crisp up as much.

Step 3: Bake them

Brush/spray with a little olive oil and optionally sprinkle some salt and bake in the oven for around 40 minutes at 350°F/175°C flipping once halfway.

If you used the par-boil method, this will be reduced, so check on them at 30 minutes.

Step 4: Season/Top the accordion potatoes

This is the best bi – choose what toppings you want to enjoy these accordion potatoes on a stick with. Check out the list above for tons of ideas, and enjoy!

Printed in Great Britain
by Amazon

14358571R00041